BUHARINOMICS

An In-Depth Study of
How President Buhari Set
Nigeria in Reverse Motion

MARTINS O. ITUA

BUHARINOMICS

To

*The memory of millions of Nigerians who have lost their
lives due to hunger, depression and Fulani Herdsmen.
May your death not be in vain as we forge ahead to create a
new Nation where we can all live in peace as one Nation
under God.*

ACKNOWLEDGEMENTS

Thank you Choice Ufouma Okoro for taking time to read the manuscript and prompting me to continue and complete the work.

A special thanks to Kamsikwa Onyinyechi Okosisi-Ezeanyika for your continued support and constructive feedback during the course of writing this book.

Ajibola Salami, I would like to thank you for your insights and fact-checking for me.

Much thanks to Fred Itua, my brother for your support throughout the course of writing this book.

Much gratitude to Malcolm Arene for taking time to read through the first manuscript and for your useful feedback.

Idris Usman, thank you for the excitement you showed when you first read the manuscript and for your support in bringing the book out.

Finally, thanks to Joseph ITIAT for the invaluable work done in converting the manuscript into a book.

I'm indebted to you all.

TABLE OF CONTENTS

BUHARINOMICS

In *Buharinomics – An In-depth Study of How President Buhari Set Nigeria in Reverse Motion*, Martins Itua has proved that no matter how far and fast falsehood has travelled, it must eventually be overtaken by truth. Truth and fact are the ingredients that Martins skilfully weaved together to come up with this work of intellectual prowess. He takes the reader through the promises made by the Buhari campaign and how those promises fell flat after the promisors got what they wanted.

He then shows, again with names, dates, places and other factual detail, how the Muhammadu Buhari administration made several unforced errors that led to the near collapse of the Nigerian economy. These actions led to a situation where Nigeria, under Buhari, had the odious distinction of being named the world headquarters for extreme poverty by the World Poverty Clock and the World Economic Forum.

I could go on and on about the facts and beautiful prose in this delightful book (delightful because, despite the saga of a collapsed economy, Martins has shown that there are still individuals in Nigeria who can say the truth to a fairly brutal dictator), but the crux of the matter is that the details in this book should serve as a guide to future Nigerian and even African leaders on how not to run an economy.

The book runs the whole gamut of the disappointment and dystopia that the era of Buharism has turned out to be. From the promises made, to the promises denied, to the reliance on 'body language' rather than well thought out policy, and to the strange habit of de-marketing Nigeria (Who can forget Muhammadu Buhari's 'lazy Nigerian youth jibe at the 2018 Commonwealth Heads of Government Meeting?), it is clear that old habits die hard. Why? Because, as Martins shows, this is a case of déjà vu. Apparently, Nigeria never learnt its 1983 lesson.

As I went through this book, the painful memories of Buhari's utterances on May 14, 2012 rang out in my mind. On that day he said, "If what happened in 2011 (alleged rigging) should again happen in 2015, by the grace of God, the dog and the baboon would all be soaked in blood."

That ought to have been a warning to Nigeria of the sort of person Buhari was. But we allowed ourselves to be hoodwinked by cleverly crafted false promises of making one Naira equal to one Dollar. We never cared to ask ourselves how a man who could not increase the size of his herd of 150 cattle would be able to increase Nigeria's Gross Domestic Product (which he ended up reducing, thus triggering a recession).

Nepotism, incompetence, failure to take responsibility and propensity for blaming others were the hallmark of Buhari's first incarnation in government. Sadly, his second coming has only shown that dictators grow old, but they do not grow into democrats.

Let me conclude with a word of advice to the readers of this brilliant work. Read this book and let it inspire you to ensure that Nigeria never goes through what she has been put through these last three and a half years. You see, history does not repeat itself. It is men that repeat history.

Reno Omokri

> *Nepotism, incompetence, failure to take responsibility and propensity for blaming others were the hallmark of Buhari's first incarnation in government. Sadly, his second coming has only shown that dictators grow old, but they do not grow into democrats.*

INTRODUCTION

That President Muhammadu Buhari is the worst thing that has ever happened to Nigeria since the amalgamation of the Southern and Northern Protectorates by Lord Lugard in 1914 is absolutely indisputable as Nigerians have never had it this rough compared to the last three and half years of Buhari's Presidency.

Buhari came to power having been dubiously packaged by Asiwaju Ahmed Bola Tinubu and co as a democrat and Nigeria's messiah to save us from the myriad of problems that were afflicting the nation. Little did Nigerians know that Buhari would amount to the worst nightmare and biggest political suicide that will eventually lead Nigeria to the undertakers. Even though there were signs during the campaign that Buhari would be an unmitigated disaster if elected, Nigerians were blindsided and hoodwinked into believing that Buhari who had truncated the democratic government of former President Shehu Shagari in December 1983 had been transformed into a democrat.

General Muhammadu Buhari, then Head of State was ably supported by Gen. Tunde Idiagbon who was second in command. During their brief period in power as Military leaders, Nigeria suffered the worst economic recession and suppression of free press. In fact, Nigerians had never seen that kind of hunger and recession as we suffered under the Military rule of Buhari where Nigerians had to queue for essential commodities such as bread and milk. It was however clear that even though Buhari was the Head of State, matters of Statecraft and Policy were often determined by his deputy, Tunde Idiagbon. Eventually, Nigeria was saved from the clutches of the Buhari Government by Gen. Ibrahim Babangida who had to reverse some of the draconian decrees of the Buhari Government and freed political prisoners who had been thrown into prison without due process.

A cursory look at the Buhari Military administration's overthrow speech of 27th August, 1985, which can be found below, establishes one major point: There is a strong resemblance between Nigeria's current woes and the issues that heralded the removal of Buhari as Nigeria's Head of State, by his lieutenants.

"I, Brigadier Joshua Nimyel Dogonyaro, of the Nigerian Army, hereby make the following declaration on behalf of my colleagues and members of the Nigerian Armed Forces.

Fellow countrymen, the intervention of the military at the end of 1983 was welcomed by the nation with unprecedented enthusiasm. Nigerians were unified in accepting the intervention and looked forward hopefully to progressive changes for the better. Almost two years later, it has become clear that the fulfilment of expectations is not forthcoming".

Brig. Dogonyaro further said, *"... No nation can ever achieve meaningful strides in its development where there is an absence of cohesion in the hierarchy of government; where it has become clear that positive action by the policy makers is hindered because as a body it lacks a unity of purpose.*

It is evident that the nation would be endangered with the risk of continuous misdirection. We are presently confronted with that danger. In such a situation, if action can be taken to arrest further damage, it should and must be taken. This is precisely what we have done.

The Nigerian public has been made to believe that the slow pace of action of the Federal Government headed by Major-General Muhammadu Buhari was due to the enormity of the problems left by the last civilian administration".

Dogonyaro further explained, ". . . *the concept of collective leadership has been substituted by stubborn and ill-advised unilateral actions, thereby destroying the principles upon which the government came to power. Any effort made to advise the leadership, met with stubborn resistance and was viewed as a challenge to authority or disloyalty.*

Thus, the scene was being set for systematic elimination of what, was termed oppositions. All the energies of the rulership were directed at this imaginary opposition rather than to effective leadership.

The result of this misdirected effort is now very evident in the country as a whole. The government has started to drift. The economy does not seem to be getting any better as we witness daily increased inflation.

The nation's meagre resources are once again being wasted on unproductive ventures. Government has distanced itself from the people and the yearnings and aspirations of the people as constantly reflected in the media have been ignored".

He concluded the speech by stating, ". . . *the initial objectives and programmes of action which were meant to have been implemented since the ascension to power of the Buhari Administration in January 1984 have been betrayed and discarded. The present state of uncertainty and stagnation cannot be permitted to degenerate into suppression and retrogression."*

Evidently, the five main reasons why Buhari was removed as Military Head of State can be summarized as follow:

1. A dictatorial lack of consultation with military colleagues.

2. Gross abuse of human rights.

3. Insensitivity to public feelings and disrespect to national leaders.

4. Abuse of power.

5. Inability to tackle the nation's economic problem.

Unfortunately, but expectedly, these are the exact same issues that Nigerians are grappling with today under the inept leadership of President Muhammadu Buhari.

This study aims to explore and critically analyse the leadership style and stewardship of President Muhammadu Buhari under the aforementioned sub themes:

1. Denial of electoral promises

2. Body language economics and de-marketing of

Nigeria

3. Gross abuse of human rights

4. Disrespect for the rule of law

5. Nepotism

6. Zero knowledge of basic economics

7. Dubious anti-corruption fight.

Furthermore, this study will also attempt to proffer solutions to the Nigerian situation, by explaining the key qualities that a Nigeria's ideal President should possess and the significance of the difficult choice that lies ahead of Nigeria, in its forthcoming 2019 general elections.

> *That President Muhammadu Buhari is the worst thing that has ever happened to Nigeria since the amalgamation of the Southern and Northern Protectorates by Lord Lugard in 1914 is absolutely indisputable as Nigerians have never had it this rough compared to the last three and half years of Buhari's Presidency.*

DENIAL OF ELECTORAL PROMISES

President Muhammadu Buhari will not only go down as Nigeria's most inept President, he will also be remembered as one of the most dubious Presidents having roundly denied all the electoral promises he made and personally signed. Nigerians had high expectations and happily voted out former President Goodluck Jonathan based on the strength of the promises that Buhari had made to them. For the benefit of people who did not have the chance to see Buhari's "My Covenant with Nigerians", I will like to share it here so that you can fully appreciate the extent of the duplicity of the APC government.

"Dear Compatriots,

In the past few months that I have travelled round this

country on campaigns, I have experienced the sheer beauty of our diversity. From Port Harcourt to Kano, from Abeokuta to Gusau, I experienced first-hand the daily sufferings and struggles of our people. I also experienced the overwhelming desire of our people for change."

Buhari further said, "*. . . the gestures of 90-year-old Hajia Fadimatu Mai Talle Tara from Kebbi State and 9-year-old Nicole Eniiyi Benson from Lagos State, who donated their life-savings to my campaign, reflect the overwhelming desire of our people for change. In their gestures, I perceived a longing for the days when honour, national pride and dignity of labour were the fundamental social principles that governed our country. As I encountered millions of our youths, who sometimes run for hours in front of my car and hanging precariously on our campaign vehicles at our state rallies, I also pondered the enormity of the task ahead. How do we give jobs to our youth? How do we reform our economy and make it work for every Nigerian?"*

He further said that if elected, he would, in his words "*lead with integrity and honour and commit myself totally to everything that is of concern to our people: security, employment, health, education, good governance and others*".

He concluded by saying, "*. . . this Covenant is to outline my agenda for Nigeria and provide a bird's eye view of how we intend to bring about the change that our country needs* *and deserves. This Covenant is derived from the manifesto of my party, the All Progressives Congress (APC). It however, represents my pledge to you all when I become your President".*

At the end of the speech, he signed it thereby in his own words, entering a covenant with Nigerians to deliver on all the promises.

For the benefit of people who didn't have the opportunity to read the different aspects of the elaborate covenant and also for the records, this study will show below the different promises in the covenant that Buhari entered with Nigerians.

1. CORRUPTION AND GOVERNANCE

No matter how vast our resources, if they are not efficiently utilized, they will only benefit a privileged few, leaving the majority in poverty. I believe if Nigeria does not kill corruption; corruption will kill Nigeria.

I pledge to:

- Publicly declare my assets and liabilities and encourage my political appointees to also publicly declare their assets and liabilities.

- Affirm that our strategy for tackling corruption

will not only focus on punishment. Rather, it will also provide incentives for disclosure and transparency.

- Show personal leadership in the war against corruption and also hold all the people who work with me to account.

- Inaugurate the National Council on Procurement as stipulated in the Procurement Act so that the Federal Executive Council, which has been turned to a weekly session of contract bazaar, will concentrate on its principal function of policy making.

- Review and implement audit recommendations by Nigeria Extractive Industries Transparency Initiative (NEITI).

- Work with the National Assembly towards the immediate enactment of a Whistle Blower Act.

- Work with the National Assembly to strengthen ICPC and EFCC by guaranteeing institutional autonomy including financial and prosecutorial independence and security of tenure of officials.

- Make the Financial Intelligence Unit (FIU) an autonomous and operational agency. Encourage proactive disclosure of information by government institutions in the spirit of the Freedom of Information Act.

- Ensure all MDAs regularly comply with their accountability responsibilities to Nigerians through the National Assembly. - Work with the leadership of the National Assembly to cut down the cost of governance. Present a national anti-corruption Strategy.

2. ACCESS TO JUSTICE AND RESPECT FOR FUNDAMENTAL HUMAN RIGHTS

One of the biggest challenges facing Nigeria is building a country that is fair to all of its citizens; a country in which all individuals feel and know that they are valued members of society with constitutionally guaranteed rights; a country that respects human dignity, promotes human development, fosters human equality and advances human freedom.

I pledge to:

- Lead a government founded on values that promote and protect fundamental human rights and freedoms. I will promote the supremacy of the Constitution and the rule of law, affirm separation of the powers of government and support an independent judiciary.

- Present a detailed strategy for protecting the fundamental rights and freedoms provided for in our Constitution. There will be emphasis on the rights of vulnerable persons including women, children and persons living with disabilities as well as access to justice and prisons reforms.

3. INSURGENCY AND INSECURITY

I have had the opportunity to serve my country in the military up to the highest level, as a Major General and as the Commander-in-Chief of the Armed Forces. In the course of my service, I had defended the territorial integrity of Nigeria. And if called upon to do so again, I shall rise to the occasion. As a father, I feel the pain of the victims of insurgency, kidnapping and violence whether they are the widows and orphans of military, paramilitary or civilians.

I pledge to:

- Ensure that under my watch, no force, external or internal, will occupy even an inch of Nigerian soil. I will give all it takes to ensure that our girls kidnapped from Chibok are rescued and reunited with their families.

- Deliver a Marshal Plan on insurgency, terrorism,

ethnic and religious violence, kidnapping, rural banditry and ensure that never again will Nigerian children be slaughtered or kidnapped at will.

- Boost the morale of our fighting forces and the generality of Nigerians by leading from the front as the Commander-in-Chief and not hide in the comfort and security of Aso Rock.

- Give especial attention to the welfare of our armed forces and all other security personnel and their families, including State-guaranteed life insurance for all officers and men as well as protect the families of our fallen heroes.

- Ensure that acts of heroism and valour in the service to the nation are publicly recognized and celebrated.

- Establish close working relationship with governors of the states affected by insurgency, with leaders of our neighbouring countries and with leaders around the world to cooperate in combating insurgency, oil theft, piracy and criminality.

- Activate regular meetings of the National Police Council to ensure the discharge of its true constitutional roles in a transparent and accountable way.

- Fight for you, and alongside you. We will fight together to defeat terrorism. But I will be honest with you about our challenges and I will bear the responsibilities of my charge. I will not lie to you or exaggerate our triumphs. My administration will be thoroughly transparent in every step of our daily struggle and together we will win the war.

4. NIGER DELTA

In many years of oil exploration, the Niger Delta has become perhaps, the world's worst eco-system, a byword for environmental degradation, exploitation and diseases. I believe that protecting the livelihood of our people in the Niger Delta should transcend our interest its oil.

I pledge to:

- Commit myself and my administration to the protection and regeneration of the environment in the Niger Delta and to ensure that oil companies comply with global best practices on environmental protection.

- Sustain and streamline the human capital development in the Niger Delta, especially focusing on youth and women.

- Reform investment in infrastructural development of the Niger Delta and ensure that the NDDC is held accountable to its mandate.

5. DIVERSITY

Nigeria's greatest asset is her people. My commitment is to invest in our people and ensure that they have the opportunity to achieve their full potentials and enjoy the full benefits of their citizenship, regardless of their religion, region, ethnicity, gender or disability.

I pledge to:

- Continually acknowledge our diversity and consciously promote equality and equity in all government businesses and activities.

- Implement the National Gender Policy including 35% of appointive positions for women.

- Work with the National Assembly to pass the National Disability Act and the Equal Opportunities Bill.

6. HEALTH

We must give real meaning to the old saying that Health is Wealth. We must take all possible measures to ensure that our people stay healthy, but we must also ensure that when they fall ill, they can get help.

Healthcare in Nigeria is in crises. Too many people do not get any treatment. For those who do get treated, all too often, the care they receive is poor. Far too many die from easily treatable diseases and what should be routine treatment often end in death. Furthermore, Nigeria is set to miss our MDG targets. The statistics speak for themselves.

I pledge to:

- Unveil a health sector review policy to ensure efficient and effective management of our health systems with focus on prevention.

- Ensure that no Nigerian will have any reason to go outside the country for medical treatment.

- Guarantee financial sustainability to the health sector and minimum basic health care for all.

- Review occupational health laws and immediately commence enforcement of the provisions to reduce hazards in the work place.

- Partner with State Governments and development partners to ensure all-round implementation of our primary health plans by expanding access to health insurance for rural communities.

7. EDUCATION

I believe that our education system must prepare our children for the responsibilities of citizenship and prepare our youths to contribute to the development of our country. Therefore, I shall focus on restoring the lost glory of our education by implementing reforms that will bring quality back into our schools and position our universities and polytechnics to provide market-relevant skills to our youths.

I pledge to:

- Embark on a program of mass mobilisation to ensure that all children of school age, no matter where they may reside in our country, and no matter the social conditions of their parents, are in school. Working in co-operation with the State Governments, we shall make the required investments in infrastructure, learning materials, nutrition and children healthcare. To this end, UBEC Fund will be reviewed to ensure greater efficiency in utilization.

- Provide on-the-job retraining opportunities for existing teachers at both the basic and secondary levels while providing the right incentives to keep teachers in the classrooms and attract bright young men and women to take up career in teaching.

- Work with other levels of government and through relevant government agencies to allocate resources to schools while strengthening community participation in school management. Implement a comprehensive review of the goal and content of our secondary education to ensure that it also serves the purpose of skills acquisition and fits purpose.

- Set up Colleges of Skills and Enterprise to replace the old technical colleges. This will be done with direct participation from relevant industry and professional groups in the private sector. Based on local market demands, each of the colleges will focus on high job demand sectors of the economy such as agriculture, ICT, telecommunications, entertainment, construction, oil and gas and sports.

- Establish special purpose fund for a Secondary School level education. Improve the competitiveness of our universities and polytechnics and position them at the heart of the national productivity, innovation and enterprise. Pursue a policy of non-discrimination between the universities and the polytechnics.

8. AGRICULTURE

Oil has served our country, but it has also excluded majority of Nigerians from the mainstream of our economy. I am convinced that our guarantee for inclusive growth is agriculture.

I pledge to:

- Make agriculture a major focus of the government and lay the institutional foundation to attract large-scale investments and capital to the sector.

- Actively promote a well-coordinated and innovatively funded Youth in Commercial Agribusiness Programme.

- Establish agricultural produce storage, pricing and marketing systems to ensure real commercial value and minimize waste.

- Work with State Governments to launch Agricultural Support Programmes that will drive agricultural land development and mechanization.

- Revamp, revitalize and improve on the national agricultural extension and rural support service system.

- Lay the groundwork for a standardized market uptake and aggregation outlets for specific agricultural produce. - Revamp the key development banks (Bank of Agriculture, Bank of Industry and Nigeria Import & Export Bank) to fund inclusive agricultural value chain operations.

- Liberalise and expand agricultural and rural insurance system with premium subventions support to farmers.

- Revamp the agricultural cooperative system to drive rural agriculture and improve stakes for smallholder farmers. - Develop a system of small-scale irrigation systems to ensure all-year round farming.

- Revamping key agriculture research institutions and deliver their outputs through effective network of extension services.

9. MANAGEMENT OF THE ECONOMY FOR PROSPERITY

Every Nigerian deserves to benefit from the running of our collective resources. We promise not to leave any Nigerian behind in our determination to create, expand and ensure equitable and effective allocation of economic opportunities. No matter the amount of funds we generate, unless there is an efficient and effective utilization, it will only create few billionaires. Unless we fight corruption, the economy will only benefit the greedy in our society.

I pledge to:

- Work with the legislature to strengthen constitutional provisions to make the meetings of the National Economic Council more periodic and predictable and its decisions more binding.

- Present annual report on the state of the economy to the National Assembly and the Nigerian People.

- The Preparation of Medium Term Expenditure Framework (MTEF) and annual Budget will be guided by job creation projections.

- Negotiate rule-based oil revenue management process, and adopt a rule based excess crude account management process, which will entail a fixed percentage (e.g. 10% or 20%) of oil revenue each year, and also set clear rules about where the proceeds will be domiciled, when the savings can be used, by whom, and what the savings can be used for.

- Work with the National Assembly to adopt a rule based, realistic and predictable oil benchmark as a basis for a more transparent management of federation account revenue and excess crude account.

- Launch a Small Business Loan Guarantee Scheme in partnership with Commercial Lenders to improve access to finance for SMEs.

- Automate the business registration process to ensure sole proprietorships can be opened within 24 hours and incorporated business within 5 days.

- Reduce the cost of company registration to a maximum of N10,000 for sole proprietorships to encourage formalization.

- Review and regulate import duty waivers to promote transparency and accountability;

- Forge partnerships with state and local governments and private sectors to promote innovation, entrepreneurship and cottage industries;

- Work with the National Assembly to review and finalize work on the Petroleum Industry Bill (PIB);

- Boost community and local participation in downstream through expansion and promotion of local content development;

- Commence organizational reforms to curb corruption in NNPC and its subsidiaries.

10. POWER

Our failure to ensure a stable supply of electricity has been an impediment to economic growth, productivity and national security.

I pledge to:

- Address the gaps in power sector privatization to ensure it serves the needs of our people.

- Explore and develop alternative sources of power such as small, medium and large hydro plants, wind, coal and solar and other forms of renewable energy to ensure efficient and affordable power supply.

- Invest in technical skills development for efficient management of energy resources.

11. SPORTS AND CULTURE

Sports and culture are important instruments for social cohesion, national integration and promotion of positive national image. They also provide a strong platform for youth development and the expression of our abundant creative talents.

I pledge to:

- Invest and encourage investments in both small and large-scale sports facilities to enable mass participation in sports.

- Ensure that participation in sports become a core component of our education at all levels.

- Activate incentives for the private sector to invest in the development of high performance sports.

Culture

I pledge to:

- Support real investments in the entertainment, arts and creative industries.

- Strengthen the regulatory framework to protect and preserve our culture and creative industry and prevent it from the scourge of piracy.

- Develop and strengthen the value link-chain of

the culture industry to deepen the industry and provide jobs.

12. YOUTH AND ICT DEVELOPMENT

The youth are the salt of the nation. More than 60% of our population is categorized as being of youth age. The future of the nation depends on the brains of the youth and not on what is buried under the ground.

I pledge to:

- Declare support for the appointment of young people with requisite qualification into key political offices to begin the incubation and mentoring for a successor political generation.

- Unveil a policy that all federal contractors must employ at least 50% young people.

- Work with the private sector to establish innovation fund for young people.

- Encourage that girls' and boys' education is prioritized in states where this is established to be a big problem.

- Review and make pronouncements, with attendant political will and commitment, on the full implementation of the national youth policy.

- Establish innovation centres in conjunction with proposed National Science Foundation and the private sector.

- Include vocational skills in the curriculum of Almajiri schools so that they become self-employed.

- Unveil a policy that will begin to multiply the efforts and effects of technology incubation centres to at least establish two of such centres in each of the geopolitical zone.

- Establish a free-tuition and scholarship scheme for pupils who have shown exceptional aptitude in science subjects at O/Levels to study ICT-related courses.

- Immediately establish linkages with friendly names to champion exchange programmes for the acquisition of IT related skills.

- Extend the local content policies to cover software and hardware developments in the youth-driven markets. Put in place a quality assurance mechanism to ensure that standards are met and adhered to and make it a policy for companies to procure a % of their ICT needs from the local market.

- Hold a summit of all ICT service providers,

OEMs, etc. both local and foreign that are doing business in Nigeria to device concrete skills transfer and capacity building models in a sustainable manner.

As indicated earlier, it is either the President simply just signed this document without reading it to fully understand that he was in fact entering a contract with Nigerians or he lacked the moral courage to accept it after winning elections and see to its full implementation. If it is true that he did not read or understand the document, it goes to further corroborate the reason for some of the biggest mistakes of his Presidency where he would simply append his signature on a list of appointees that is filled with names of dead people.

On the other hand, if he lacked the moral courage to accept the fact that he had in fact signed a contract with Nigerians, it would mean that he is duplicitous and cannot be trusted. It would also mean that his much-touted integrity and incorruptibility is only word of mouth and have no practical relevance.

It would seem that Nigerians were so much in a hurry to push out President Goodluck Jonathan that they didn't bother to interrogate the then Presidential Candidate Muhammadu Buhari on how he intends to accomplish the humongous task that he set for himself. It is also clear that APC capitalized on the fact that the largest voting bloc of the populace i.e. Northern Nigeria, are either illiterates or have minimal education.

It is also on record that during the South East Presidential rally at Dan Anyiam Stadium, Owerri, then APC Candidate Presidential Buhari, declared to the people that he would make the Naira equal to the Dollar (USD) in value if elected into office. However, in more recent times, despite evidence to the contrary, Buhari has vehemently denied making such a promise.

President Muhammadu Buhari will not only go down as Nigeria's most inept President, he will also be remembered as one of the most dubious Presidents having roundly denied all the electoral promises he made and personally signed ... It is either the President simply just signed this document without reading it to fully understand that he was in fact entering a contract with Nigerians or he lacked the moral courage to accept it after winning elections and see to its full implementation.

BUHARI'S BODY LANGUAGE AND CONSTANT DEMARKETING OF NIGERIA

President Buhari, on assumption of office took the definition of body language to a whole new level as he would be completely mute on critical issues regarding the country and the well-being of Nigerians. People believed he performed miracles in the power sector when he came into office, as Nigerians seemed to be enjoying better power supply. This was despite the fact he hadn't done anything either by way of policy or improvement in infrastructure to change the situation.

In the first six months of his administration, Nigerians knew nothing about what he was thinking about or doing as there was nothing to indicate his policy direction. It is believed that

Buhari's uncertain body language and lack of clarity in policy were major reasons why the value of the Naira plummeted and the economy going into recession. While Buhari was carrying himself about as a demi-god of some sort in Aso Rock, foreign investors were petrified and quickly withdrew their capital investments in the country. Observant Nigerians, policy makers and investors understood that there is no such thing as body language in the formulation and implementation of policy.

President Buhari believed that he could continue to

In the first six months of his administration, Nigerians knew nothing about what he was thinking about or doing as there was nothing to indicate his policy direction. It is believed that Buhari's uncertain body language and lack of clarity in policy were major reasons why the value of the Naira plummeted and the economy going into recession. While Buhari was carrying himself about as a demi-god of some sort in Aso Rock, foreign investors were petrified and quickly withdrew their capital investments in the country.

govern by himself without a cabinet who will have the responsibility to man the different ministries. While he was prevaricating and dillydallying on whether to appoint ministers or not, the economy was in reverse gear and by the time he eventually decided to appoint his ministers, it was too late to salvage the economy, as the Naira was in a free-fall. It is something the President should be thoroughly ashamed of; that while he inherited an economy with a GDP of over $500 billion in May 2015 and value of the Naira exchanging for less than N200 to one USD, he simply folded his hands and allowed the economy slide into recession. By the time the President woke up from his slumber and indecision, Nigeria's economy had haemorrhaged irredeemably.

Clearly, three and half years down the line, President Buhari is still unable to understand that however good his body language may be, it can only have negative unintended consequences. Moreover, Nigerians are neither professionals in studying body language nor have the patience to study body language.

> *President Buhari believed that he could continue to govern by himself without a cabinet who will have the responsibility to man the different ministries. While he was prevaricating and dillydallying on whether to appoint ministers or not, the economy was in reverse gear and by the time he eventually decided to appoint his ministers, it was too late to salvage the economy, as the Naira was in a free-fall. It is something the President should be thoroughly ashamed of; that while he inherited an economy with a GDP of over $500 billion in May 2015 and value of the Naira exchanging for less than N200 to one USD, he simply folded his hands and allowed the economy slide into recession. By the time the President woke up from his slumber and indecision, Nigeria's economy had haemorrhaged irredeemably.*

PRESIDENT BUHARI AS CHIEF DE-MARKETER INSTEAD OF MARKETER-IN-CHIEF

Former British Prime Minister David Cameron was famously overheard telling Queen Elizabeth II that Afghanistan and Nigeria were "fantastically corrupt countries," and "possibly the two most corrupt countries in the world."

When President Buhari was asked if Nigeria was "fantastically corrupt," our President in the full glare of the world responded: "Yes." Prompted further, he said "I am not going to demand any apology from anybody."

In his mind, he probably believed that he was being honest, but he didn't realize that he was simply washing Nigeria's dirty linen in public. He was telling the whole world that Nigeria is a nation of crooks and criminals. How could he possibly think that on the one hand, he tells the whole world that Nigerians are thieves and on the other hand, he wants investors to come to Nigeria to invest their money? It is similar to a father who is praying for his daughter to get married while he climbs the roof top at the same time, announcing to every potential suitor that his daughter is a prostitute.

President Buhari has used a good number of his foreign travels to hurt Nigeria's reputation on the international stage. Only recently, at a business forum of Commonwealth Heads of Government in London, the President, while responding to a question, told the whole world that "Nigeria's youth do nothing and want everything for free. A lot of them haven't been to school and they are claiming, you know, that, Nigeria has been an oil producing country therefore they should sit and do nothing and get housing, healthcare, education free". Thereby asserting that Nigerian youths are lazy.

President Buhari will go down in history and probably also enter Guinness Book of World Records as the first and only President in the world who has a penchant for speaking badly about his citizens while outside the country. How he arrived at the conclusion that Nigerian youths are lazy is questionable; if he was more in tune with the pulse of the nation, he would have known that Nigerian youths are exceedingly talented and probably the most hardworking in Africa.

Our youths have managed to eke out a living despite the failure of leadership and lack of basic infrastructure in the country. A visit to Lagos, Aba,

> *President Buhari will go down in history and probably also enter Guinness Book of World Records as the first and only President in the world who has a penchant for speaking badly about his citizens while outside the country.*

Onitsha, Benin, Nnewi, FCT, Kano, etc. will convince anyone that Nigerian youths are fighting against the odds daily in order to make their lives better and bring positive change to the country that has failed them time and time again. It is therefore beyond scandalous and totally unprecedented that the President will go to the United Kingdom, and publicly castigate and denigrate Nigerian youths and an entire generation as lazy.

President Buhari had another opportunity during the recent visit of the German Chancellor Angela

> *Our youths have managed to eke out a living despite the failure of leadership and lack of basic infrastructure in the country. A visit to Lagos, Aba, Onitsha, Benin, Nnewi, FCT, Kano, etc. will convince anyone that Nigerian youths are fighting against the odds daily in order to make their lives better and bring positive change to the country that has failed them time and time again. It is therefore beyond scandalous and totally unprecedented that the President will go to the United Kingdom, and publicly castigate and denigrate Nigerian youths and an entire generation as lazy.*

Merkel to extol the virtues of Nigeria's youths but however, yet again, he chose to focus on the negatives. Hear him: "I guess many of my country men and women illegally struggle to find their way to European countries through the deserts and the Mediterranean because they feel there are greener pastures there whether they are prepared for it or not. As an administration, we are not in support of it . . . about three weeks ago, we repatriated 3,000 Nigerians from Libya. They want to travel to Europe illegally. We do not support this and anybody caught is at his or her own risk . . . any Nigerian found in Libya or anywhere on his way to Europe through illegal means will be brought home and we will send him back to the local government."

The bigger question is why does President Buhari enjoy putting Nigerians under the bus at every given opportunity? The most obvious answer is that the President is totally disconnected from the people that he supposedly governs. It is crystal clear that the President has never really engaged with Nigerians and does not understand the sheer difficulty that Nigerians daily face in an environment where there is a glaring failure of leadership and lack of basic social services.

> *The bigger question is why does President Buhari enjoy putting Nigerians under the bus at every given opportunity? The most obvious answer is that the President is totally disconnected from the people that he supposedly governs. It is crystal clear that the President has never really engaged with Nigerians and does not understand the sheer difficulty that Nigerians daily face in an environment where there is a glaring failure of leadership and lack of basic social services.*

Another possible explanation is that President Buhari has an inferiority complex whenever he is amongst Western Leaders.

Imagine President Buhari standing next to President Donald Trump and asked his comments about Trump's remarks that African countries are a 'shithole'. His response was: "I'm very careful with what the press says about [people] other than myself. I'm not sure about the validity or whether that allegation against the president was true or not. So the best thing for me is to keep quiet." Yes, it is possible that one would say he wanted to be diplomatic, but the truth is that he missed an opportunity to stand tall in defence of all African countries.

Again, President Buhari while standing next to Chancellor Angela Merkel in Germany was prompted with a response to his wife, Mrs. Aisha Buhari's comments that she might not back her husband at the next election unless he got a grip on his government. The President's response was, "I don't know which party my wife belongs to, but she belongs to my kitchen and my living room and the other room." How does the President of a country say, in the presence of another world leader, that the place of his wife is in the bedroom? Pastor Tunde Bakare of Latter Rain Assembly, who had been running mate to Buhari in a previous election had a sharp rebuke for the President as follows:

"Whatever makes a man to look at his wife and say she is only good for the kitchen, the living room and the other room shows you what goes on in the mind of a leader … our President was standing next to the most powerful woman in the world and reduced the African woman to just the kitchen and the bedroom. I stand here to say that women are not objects to be used but persons to be respected…"

Bakare further said, ". . . if that was meant to be a joke by the President, then, that is just an expensive joke that is uncalled for on an international scene. It was unnecessary and an embarrassment to even the mothers that bore us and the daughters that we are raising . . . their place is not just in the bedroom or kitchen; their place is also in the parliament and one day, who knows, the day will come that even the Villa will be occupied by a woman in this country."

Pastor Bakare's rebuke of the President reflected the total outrage and utter dismay of the entire civilized world against the President's misogyny and parochialism. It is quite shocking and disappointing that the President of the world's biggest Black Country and Africa's largest economy would simply dismiss and confine his wife to the kitchen and bedroom.

GROSS ABUSE OF HUMAN RIGHTS

Instances of human rights abuses under Buhari's administrations, both as a civilian President and Military Head of State, have been unrivalled in Nigeria's history.

It is important to commend the National Assembly for refusing to grant President Buhari's request for "Emergency Economic Bill", as that would have effectively given him summary powers and moved the country from a democratic government to a dictatorship. In addition, it would have led to the death of the National Assembly, as they would have been unable to check the excesses of the Executive arm of government. It would have also meant that the Buhari administration can bypass and abuse the Procurement Act, which requires public advertisement and bidding for all contracts. Nigeria is eternally gratefully to the National Assembly, for its doggedness in refusing to be bullied into acceptance, as that would have led the nation into total anarchy where only the President's cronies will be favoured in the award of contracts.

> *It is important to commend the National Assembly for refusing to grant President Buhari's request for "Emergency Economic Bill", as that would have effectively given him summary powers and moved the country from a democratic government to a dictatorship. In addition, it would have led to the death of the National Assembly, as they would have been unable to check the excesses of the Executive arm of government. It would have also meant that the Buhari administration can bypass and abuse the Procurement Act, which requires public advertisement and bidding for all contracts.*

Below are some well publicised incidents of gross abuse of human rights, under the Buhari administration:

KADUNA MASSACRE OF 350 MEMBERS OF SHIITE SECT

According to Amnesty International, the Nigerian Military committed mass murder and used unlawful excessive force in clashes with members of a Shiite sect.

The Nigerian Army clashed with members of the Islamic Movement in Nigeria (IMN) led by Ibrahim el-Zakzaky between December 12 and 14, 2015, in Kaduna state, Northern Nigeria. According to the Nigerian Army, the clashes began after IMN members attempted to assassinate Nigeria's Chief of Army Staff but the IMN claims that it was an unprovoked attack by the army.

Amnesty International reports, "More than 350 people are believed to have been unlawfully killed by the military between 12 and 14 December, following a confrontation between members of the Islamic Movement of Nigeria (IMN) and soldiers in Zaria, Kaduna state."

Some members of the Islamic Movement of Nigeria

were carrying batons, knives, and machetes and had refused to clear the road near their headquarters for the military convoy to pass. In return, the soldiers opened fire indiscriminately killing over 350 people including children.

Amnesty International concluded, ". . . it is clear that the military not only used unlawful and excessive force against men, women and children, unlawfully killing hundreds, but then made considerable efforts to try to cover-up these crimes".

President Buhari till date, is yet to hold the Army to account or bring any offender to book. Furthermore, the leader of Islamic Movement of Nigeria, el-Zakzaky and his wife Zeinat el-Zakzaky, have been detained without trial or access to legal representation, despite the ruling of a Federal High Court in Abuja ordering their release.

OPERATION PYTHON DANCE AND KILLING OF OVER 100 INDEPENDENT PEOPLE OF BIAFRA (IPOB) SUPPORTERS

According to Igbo Civil Society Coalition (ICSCO), activists, human rights groups and several eye witnesses, the Nigeria army killed over 100 and injured over 200 others during an Army operation called Operation Python Dance in the South East of Nigeria. These people were killed in cold blood and their bodies either dumped in the forest or buried in mass graves by the Nigerian Army.

Since these unwarranted killings by the Nigerian Army in September 2017, President Buhari has carried on business as usual, while the families of those affected are left to lick their wounds. It is however commendable that the International Court of Justice (ICJ) at the Hague, is set to investigate the killings, following a report by Nigerian CNN award winning journalist, Mr. Ahaoma Kanu.

FAILURE TO RELEASE FORMER NATIONAL SECURITY ADVISER, COL. SAMBO DASUKI

President Buhari's penchant for abuse of human rights is further demonstrated by his wilful and deliberate refusal to release former National Security Adviser, Col. Sambo Dasuki (Rtd), despite being granted bail by different courts as follows:

1. 30th August 2015, Dasuki was first granted bail by Adeniyi Ademola, then presiding judge of the

Federal Capital Territory (FCT) in Abuja, only to be immediately rearrested at the gates of Kuje prison.

2. 18th December 2015, Dasuki was again granted bail by Hussein Baba Yusuf, Justice of the FCT High court but it was denied.

3. October 2016, the ECOWAS Court also ordered the federal government to pay a compensation of N15 million to Dasuki for his "unlawful arrest".

4. 24th January 2017, Yusuf reaffirmed the bail on Dasuki on the grounds that he was entitled to it and having being admitted to same since 2015 when the federal government brought criminal charges against him. Yet, he was denied.

5. 5th April 2017, Ahmed Mohammed, presiding judge of FCT high court, reaffirmed the 2015 bail granted Dasuki after hearing the ex-NSA's appeal of the amended seven-count charge against him.

6. 18th May 2018, Yusuf further reaffirmed the bail he granted Dasuki in 2015.

7. 2nd July 2018, Ijeoma Ojukwu, the Presiding Judge, described Dasuki's continuous detention as an aberration to the rule of law.

President Buhari either does not understand what human rights mean and why they should not be trampled upon, or he doesn't care. The antecedents of the President clearly show that respecting the rights and dignity of Nigeria's citizens, are the last things on his list.

As Military Head of State, Gen. Buhari and his cohorts were probably the most notorious and unprosecuted violators of human rights in the history of Nigeria. Immediately after overthrowing the government of Shehu Shagari in December 1983,

> *President Buhari either does not understand what human rights mean and why they should not be trampled upon, or he doesn't care. The antecedents of the President clearly show that respecting the rights and dignity of Nigeria's citizens, are the last things on his list.*

Gen. Buhari promulgated the infamous Decree Number Four of 1984 which gave them power against the Nigerian press. Eventually, his government executed Bernard Ogedengbe, Bartholomew Owoh and Lawal Ojulope, despite public pleas. In fact, they were executed, following a retroactive decree by the Buhari government. This decree is considered by scholars, as the most repressive law ever enacted in Nigeria.

Buhari government's Decree Number Two made it possible for his government to detain anybody, whether such person is a citizen of the country or foreigner. In essence, the decree did not recognize the significance of the judiciary but was merely interested in achieving its aims of dictatorial tendencies. It was this law that enabled his government to hound and make ridiculous prison sentences of up to 125 years to perceived political enemies and politicians.

There are certain people who are hoping that President Buhari may have changed his ways and become a democrat. But his secon'd coming as Nigeria's civilian President has proved that an old dog cannot learn new tricks. It is in the DNA of the President to trample on the rights and dignity of Nigerians. Or how else can anyone explain that the Nigerian Army have killed hundreds of people – including women and children who were unable to defend themselves? These perpetrators and harbingers of evil were hailed and even rewarded instead of being investigated and punished.

It is absolutely clear that President Buhari is

inherently unable to provide leadership in a modern and civilized society where he needs to respect human rights and the dignity of fellow Nigerians. Nigerians are not animals who need to be hounded, dragged, beaten or killed. The recent quest for the National Assembly to enact a law on Hate Speech further validates this point that President Buhari is only interested in taking Nigeria to the days of Decree 4 of 1984.

> *It is absolutely clear that President Buhari is inherently unable to provide leadership in a modern and civilized society where he needs to respect human rights and the dignity of fellow Nigerians. Nigerians are not animals who need to be hounded, dragged, beaten or killed. The recent quest for the National Assembly to enact a law on Hate Speech further validates this point that President Buhari is only interested in taking Nigeria to the days of Decree 4 of 1984.*

CHAPTER 4

DISRESPECT FOR THE RULE OF LAW

It is not certain whether President Buhari has ever fully read the Constitution of the Federal Republic of Nigeria, but it is easy to deduce from his actions, that he clearly does not understand the supremacy of the constitution and that any other law is null and void to the extent that they are inconsistent with the constitution. The Constitution is the number one law and its supremacy is emphasised in Section 1(1) of the Constitution, where it says, "the constitution is supreme and binding on every person in the Country."

Nigeria's supreme law is not determined or affected by the President's body language and whether he likes a section of the law or not, is a non-issue. For instance, our constitution says that we have three arms of government, namely: The Executive, the Legislature and the Judiciary, the existence of which is supposed to prevent possible abuse of authority. In essence, the legislature has the power to make laws, the executive branch has the authority to administer and enforce the law, while the judiciary tries cases brought before the courts and interprets the law.

The President is not permitted to cherry-pick what laws to obey and follow, depending on his likes and dislikes. At a recent Annual Conference of the Nigerian Bar Association, where President Buhari was the guest of honour, the President told the gathering of senior lawyers and judges that his administration will, in his words, ". . . prioritise national security over and above the rule of law". He reportedly said, "The rule of law must be subject to the supremacy of the nation's security and national interest. Our apex court has had cause to adopt a position on this issue in this regard and it is now a matter of judicial recognition that where national security and public interest are threatened or there is a likelihood of their being threatened, the individual rights of those allegedly responsible must take second place, in favour of the greater

> *The President is not permitted to cherry-pick what laws to obey and follow, depending on his likes and dislikes. At a recent Annual Conference of the Nigerian Bar Association, where President Buhari was the guest of honour, the President told the gathering of senior lawyers and judges that his administration will, in his words, "…prioritise national security over and above the rule of law".*

good of society".

This unfortunate statement by the President, is reminiscent of Germany under Adolf Hitler, which later gave him summary powers to suppress free press and throw innocent people into concentration camps.

Further, this kind of statement by the President, underscores the fact that he needs a crash course in constitutional law and that the constitution is the supreme law of the land and we become a banana republic when we cherry-pick which laws to obey. And to imagine that he made this sacrilegious statement in a gathering of eminent lawyers, further confirms the utter contempt our President has for the constitution of the Federal Republic of Nigeria.

It is this warped understanding and interpretation of the supremacy of the constitution that makes the President think he has the right to deny bail to former National Security Adviser, Col. Sambo Dasuki, despite the fact that the courts have granted him bail six times, including the one granted by the West African Court. It is also clear that this kind of mind-set is responsible for the President's refusal to release the leader of the Shi'ites Movement, Ibrahim el-Zakzaky and his wife.

Reacting to the President's open attack on the Nation's constitution, Lagos lawyer Ebun-Olu Adegboruwa said the rule of law is sacrosanct. In his words, "... the rule of law limits and interposes upon the rule of self all forms of arbitrariness and is thus preferable to the whims and caprices of individuals . . ." He warned that a stance like Buhari's should be avoided, particularly in the light of March 2019 elections. Adegboruwa went further and said, "It is a dangerous proposition as we approach 2019. Taken to its proper interpretation, it may be taken to be an advance notice to the

> *This kind of statement by the President, underscores the fact that he needs a crash course in constitutional law and that the constitution is the supreme law of the land and we become a banana republic when we cherry-pick which laws to obey. And to imagine that he made this sacrilegious statement in a gathering of eminent lawyers, further confirms the utter contempt our President has for the constitution of the Federal Republic of Nigeria.*
>
> *It is this warped understanding and interpretation of the supremacy of the constitution that makes the President think he has the right to deny bail to former National Security Adviser, Col. Sambo Dasuki, despite the fact that the courts have granted him bail six times, including the one granted by the West African Court. It is also clear that this kind of mind-set is responsible for the President's refusal to release the leader of the Shi'ites Movement, Ibrahim el-Zakzaky and his wife.*

people of Nigeria, to brace up for likely threats to their rights and liberties, in the coming days".

Following this utterance, Nigeria's opposition party, the People's Democratic Party 'PDP' had a sharp rebuke for the President, stating, "Our national interest is thoroughly embedded, protected, expressed and enforced only under the rule of law as provided by our constitution and there is no how Nigerians can allow an individual to superimpose or override the Constitution with his personal whims and impulses".

They further said, "President Buhari should therefore be made to answer for the litany of human rights violations in Nigeria, including documented disobedience to court orders, extra-judicial and arbitrary executions, unlawful arrests and political detentions, killing of persons in custody, torture and excessive use of force by security forces on innocent citizens."

The Nobel Laureate, Prof. Wole Soyinka had this to say: "Here we go again! At his first coming, it was 'I intend to tamper with Freedom of the Press' and Buhari did proceed to suit action to the words, sending two journalists, Irabor and Thompson, to prison as a reward for their professional integrity ... He further affirmed, "...now, a vague, vaporous, but commodious concept dubbed 'national interest' is being trotted out as alibi for flouting the decisions of the Nigerian judiciary."

I'm going to cite other instances where it was clear that President has no respect for the rule of law and really does not care what Nigerians think or say about him.

DSS OPERATIVES INVADING HOMES OF SENIOR JUDGES AT DEAD OF THE NIGHT

In October 2016, the entire Nation awoke to the shocking news of the invasion of the homes of senior judges, by men of the Department of Secret Service (DSS). This was intended to be a sting operation and was carried in a manner that criminalised the accused judges. This operation was promptly condemned by all well-meaning Nigerians, as it was seen as an open attack on the Judiciary and outright desecration of the temple of justice. Those raided included the current Chief Justice of the Federation, Justice Walter Onnoghen and Sylvanus Ngwuta and Justices Adeniyi Ademola, Muazu Pindiga and Nnamdi Dimgba of the Federal High Court.

This raid by the DSS further confirmed what Nigerians already knew, that President Buhari has utter disrespect for the rule of law and principle of separation of powers. To him, power is only an instrument of control and harassment of perceived enemies. It is clear that the President lacks the temperament to preside over Nigeria in a democratic setting and given the opportunity, he will end up as a despot and tyrant unable to stand the opposition.

DSS INVASION OF THE NATIONAL ASSEMBLY

It seemed like a Military coup when operatives of the DSS, with covered faces, invaded the gates of the National Assembly and prevented members of the national Parliament from gaining access into the compound. This was unprecedented in the history of Nigeria; that the Secret Service under the instruction of a 'higher authority' will take over the premises of the third arm of government. It was roundly condemned by all well-meaning Nigerians

> *It is clear that the President lacks the temperament to preside over Nigeria in a democratic setting and given the opportunity, he will end up as a despot and tyrant unable to stand the opposition.*

and the head of the DSS was fired for the invasion which caused the Nation a huge embarrassment as it was beamed in the glare of the whole world.

In a normal situation where the rule of law is supreme, these officials and their boss would be arrested by the Police and tried for treason as that attack was not only against the third arm of government but a grave danger to our democracy.

Sadly, they walked away free.

NEPOTISM IN VIOLATION OF THE CONSTITUTION

At the United States Institute of Peace (USIP), on 22nd July 2015, shortly before the newly sworn-in President Buhari was to give a speech covering security and counterterrorism issues in Nigeria and West Africa, members of the audience were invited to ask him questions in a session moderated by former United Nations Secretary of State for African Affairs, Johnnie Carson.

Dr. Pauline Baker, the President Emeritus of The Fund for Peace, asked a question and inquired about security in the Niger Delta area. Her exact enquiry was, ". . . My question relates to another area of Nigeria that hasn't gotten a lot of attention during this trip and that is the Niger Delta. It's a challenge that you are going to face. I wonder if you would tell us how you intend to approach it with particular reference to the amnesty, bunkering, and inclusive development"

At first, the President struggled to understand the question and the moderator tried to explain to him the meaning of the word 'inclusive'. Then to the utter amazement and dismay of the audience, Nigerians and the whole world, President Buhari opened his mouth and declared the famous mathematical puzzle of 97% and 5% as follows:

"I hope you have a copy of the election results. The constituents, for example, that gave me 97% cannot in all honesty be treated on some issues with constituencies that gave me 5%".

That was typical, and that mind-set eventually defined his entire Presidency, where his worldview is defined by his backyard and not the entire country. One of the first things President Buhari did was to appoint the Acting Chairperson of Independent Electoral Commission, after the expiration of the term of Prof. Attahiru Jega. He proceeded and appointed Mrs. Amina Zakari whose late father was the former Emir of Kazaure and was married to President Buhari's elder sister. It was also confirmed that President Buhari lived with and spent a significant part of his early years in the home of Amina Zakari's father.

PRINCIPLE OF FEDERAL CHARACTER UNDER 1999 CONSTITUTION

It is important we remind the President that he is bound by the Constitution of the Federal Republic of Nigeria in Section 14, subsection 3 which states:

"The composition of the Government of the Federation or any of its agencies and the conduct of its affairs shall be carried out in such a manner to reflect the federal character of Nigeria and the need to promote national unity, and also to command national loyalty thereby ensuring that there shall be no predominance of persons from a few states or from a few ethnic of other sectional groups in that government or in any of its agencies".

The framers of the Nigerian constitution must have envisaged the possibility of a preponderance of people from a particular region or religious background in federal appointments. Hence, it became a part of the constitution and its purpose is to ensure true representation and national integration.

This is the reason for my earlier assertion that either

President Buhari has never read the constitution of the Federal Republic of Nigeria or he does not understand it or does not care whether he upholds it or not. It should have been clear to him, that appointing only people from his region into critical and sensitive positions in government, is nepotism and violates the constitution to which he swore.

Of course, there is the argument that federal appointments should solely be on the basis of merit, rather than on strict application of the federal character principle. While this argument is valid, it must however be emphasised, that there is an abundance of human resources and qualified people in all parts of Nigeria and it makes no sense

> *Of course, there is the argument that federal appointments should solely be on the basis of merit, rather than on strict application of the federal character principle. While this argument is valid, it must however be emphasised, that there is an abundance of human resources and qualified people in all parts of Nigeria and it makes no sense to pretend that there are only qualified people from one ethnic stock.*

to pretend that there are only qualified people from one ethnic stock.

President Buhari is clearly more comfortable with people who share his religion and language and come from the same region. This would explain why he has concentrated the entire security apparatchiks and other sensitive appointments in the hands of his brothers from the Northern part of Nigeria. It is also likely that he would rather have them speak in Hausa during their security meetings, as they are from the same region and belong to the same religion.

Position	Region	Religion
Chief of Army Staff	North	Muslim
Chief of Naval Staff	South	Christian
Chief of Air force Staff	North	Muslim
Chief of Defence Staff	South	Christian
Chairman of EFCC	North	Muslim
Commandant of NSCDC	North	Muslim
Inspector General of Police	North	Muslim
National Security Adviser	North	Muslim
DG of Department of State Security	North	Muslim
Comptroller of Nigeria Immigration Service	North	Muslim
Comptroller of Customs	North	Muslim
Head of Fire Service	North	Muslim
DG of NEMA	North	Muslim
Director of National Intelligence Agency	North	Muslim
Marshall of FRSC	South	Christian
Ministry of Interior	North	Muslim
Ministry of Defence	North	Muslim
Independent Electoral Commission INEC	North	Muslim
NNPC	North	Muslim

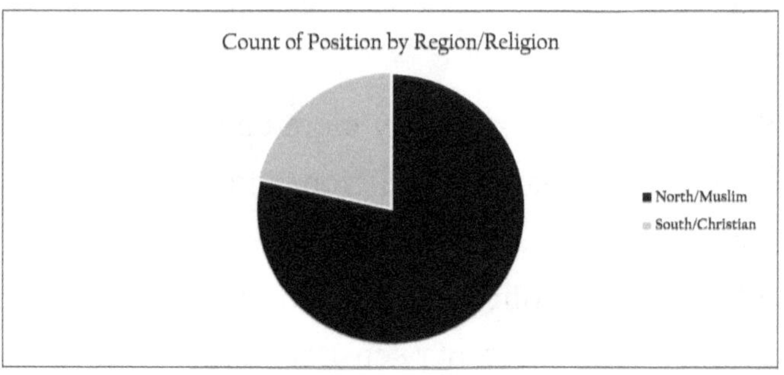

Looking at the obvious concentration of people from the Northern part of Nigeria in President Buhari's appointments in critical offices, one cannot but agree with the dispassionate assessment of former President Olusegun Obasanjo in describing Buhari's administration as, ". . . nepotic deployment, bordering on clannishness". All Nigerians, irrespective of religious and ethnic affiliations agree that President Buhari's nepotism and brazen affront on Nigeria's constitution is unprecedented and unrivalled.

Only recently, the former Director-General of the Department of Secret Service – Mr. Lawal Daura, was fired by Vice President Yemi Osibanjo due to several infractions, including the invasion of the National Assembly. Of course, it was clear that this was only possible because the President was out of the country at the time. It was expected that

President Buhari would reverse the appointment and he didn't disappoint as he went and fished out Mr. Yusuf Magaji Bichi who had retired from Service since February 2017 and appointed him as the DG of the DSS. Yusuf Bichi is from Kano State.

It should be clear to everyone who cares about the unity and peaceful co-existence of Nigeria, that President Buhari's Northernisation agenda is inimical to national integration.

The rise of the Independent People of Biafra 'IPOB' and their agitation for independence is a direct result of feelings of marginalization and over-

> *Looking at the obvious concentration of people from the Northern part of Nigeria in President Buhari's appointments in critical offices, one cannot but agree with the dispassionate assessment of former President Olusegun Obasanjo in describing Buhari's administration as, "… nepotic deployment, bordering on clannishness". All Nigerians, irrespective of religious and ethnic affiliations agree that President Buhari's nepotism and brazen affront on Nigeria's constitution is unprecedented and unrivalled.*

concentration of power in one section of the country. These feelings of marginalization will not go away, even if President Buhari decides to kill all the agitators using Nigeria's military for as long as people do not feel a sense of belonging to Nigeria. President Buhari ought to know better, having fought in the civil war of 1967 to 1970 between Biafra and Nigeria but he rather chose to ignore the lessons of history.

> *It should be clear to everyone who cares about the unity and peaceful co-existence of Nigeria, that President Buhari's Northernisation agenda is inimical to national integration.*

President Buhari's evil and unconstitutional 97% vs. 5% formula and mindset, is the reason why Nigeria is on the precipice today and at the verge of conflagration. It is clear that he neither cares about the constitution of Nigeria nor the feelings of the larger population, as he has clearly made himself the President of Northern Nigeria who apparently gave him 97% of votes compared with the other parts who collectively gave him only 5%. The verdict must be clear that President Buhari is an irredeemable ethnocentric bigot who does not mean well for Nigeria and no amount of white-wash can change the person that he is and what he represents.

> *President Buhari's evil and unconstitutional 97% vs. 5% formula and mindset, is the reason why Nigeria is on the precipice today and at the verge of conflagration. It is clear that he neither cares about the constitution of Nigeria nor the feelings of the larger population, as he has clearly made himself the President of Northern Nigeria who apparently gave him 97% of votes compared with the other parts who collectively gave him only 5%. The verdict must be clear that President Buhari is an irredeemable ethnocentric bigot who does not mean well for Nigeria and no amount of white-wash can change the person that he is and what he represents.*

ZERO KNOWLEDGE
OF BASIC ECONOMICS

Former President Obasanjo had given his candid opinion to Nigerians about the candidate Muhammadu Buhari prior to the elections of 2015. Of Buhari he said, "…he was weak in the knowledge and understanding of the economy. . ." However, Obasanjo had ignored the fact that many of our problems have resulted from poorly managed economy and bad policies.

When the then Candidate Buhari made a promise while campaigning in Owerri, that he would ensure that the Naira was equal to the dollar in value, if voted into office, it was clear that he lacked knowledge of how economies function. No matter how bad the Nigeria's educational system has become, it is impossible for even a secondary school leaver who passed Ordinary Level Economics to make such a blunder, as the value of currency does not respond to vain promises and administrative fiat, but to sound economic policies.

President Buhari must be utterly shocked that his hollow promise of reviving the economy didn't have any basis in economic theory, as the value of the Naira jumped from less than N200 to one USD, to as high as N500 to one USD. In fact, under his watch, the nation plunged into recession in the first year of his administration, while the issues of fuel scarcity, forex scarcity, devaluation of the naira with higher

When the then Candidate Buhari made a promise while campaigning in Owerri, that he would ensure that the Naira was equal to the dollar in value, if voted into office, it was clear that he lacked knowledge of how economies function. No matter how bad the Nigeria's educational system has become, it is impossible for even a secondary school leaver who passed Ordinary Level Economics to make such a blunder, as the value of currency does not respond to vain promises and administrative fiat, but to sound economic policies.

inflation and massive job losses, crippled the economic fortunes of many families.

NIGERIA BECOMES WORLD POVERTY CAPITAL

Right under President Buhari's watch and while blaming past administrations, studies by Brookings Institute, have confirmed that Nigeria has overtaken India as the country with the largest number of people living in extreme poverty, with an estimated 87 million Nigerians, or around half of the country's population, thought to be living on less than $1.90 a day. Nigeria has higher poverty levels than war-torn Democratic Republic of Congo. The study further confirmed that extreme poverty in Nigeria is growing by six people every minute, while poverty in India continues to fall.

British Prime Minister, Theresa May, during her

> *Under his watch, the nation plunged into recession in the first year of his administration, while the issues of fuel scarcity, forex scarcity, devaluation of the naira with higher inflation and massive job losses, crippled the economic fortunes of many families.*

recent visit to Nigeria further confirmed that Nigeria is home to the highest number of very poor people in the world.

But the truth is that Nigerians didn't need the Brookings Institute study or the British Prime Minister to confirm what they already knew, as the three times life was this difficult in Nigeria, was during the Nigerian civil war of 1967-1970, Buhari's tenure as Military Head of State from January 1984 to August 1985 and now under same President Buhari in a civilian government.

It is good to remind Nigerians with a quote from the first speech by Gen. Ibrahim Babangida (Rtd.), after he overthrew the government of Buhari in August 1985. In his words, "With the nation at the mercy of political misdirection and on the brink of economic collapse, a new sense of hope was created in the minds of every Nigerian. Since January 1984, however, we have witnessed a systematic denigration of that hope. It was stated then that mismanagement of political leadership and a general deterioration in the standard of living, which had subjected the common man to intolerable suffering, were the reasons for the intervention…"

Babangida further said, ". . . unemployment has

Right under President Buhari's watch and while blaming past administrations, studies by Brookings Institute, have confirmed that Nigeria has overtaken India as the country with the largest number of people living in extreme poverty, with an estimated 87 million Nigerians, or around half of the country's population, thought to be living on less than $1.90 a day. Nigeria has higher poverty levels than war-torn Democratic Republic of Congo. The study further confirmed that extreme poverty in Nigeria is growing by six people every minute, while poverty in India continues to fall.

stretched to critical dimensions. Due to the stalemate, which arose in negotiation with the International Monetary Fund, the former government embarked on a series of counter-trade agreements. Under the counter-trade agreements, Nigerians were forced to buy goods and commodities at higher prices than obtained in the international market."

The ugly scenario above is over 30 years ago that

Nigerians were saved from the hands of Gen. Buhari and it's a clear reminder of the same issues that Nigerians are grappling with today.

1. UNEMPLOYMENT

According to the National Bureau of Statistics, out of a total active labour force of 85.08 million people in Nigeria, about 16 million people were unemployed in the third quarter of 2017. These figures are probably much higher than that, as millions of Nigerians have been thrown into the labour market since the advent of the current Buhari government. The business environment under this government has been hostile to the extent that millions of people have shut down their businesses, which has led to many more millions of people losing their means of livelihoods. The British Prime Minister further confirmed that. In her words, "… 87 million Nigerians live below $1 and 90 cents a day, making it home to more very poor people than any other nation in the world".

President Buhari has succeeded in reducing Nigeria to a level where we are now being compared with war-torn Democratic Republic of Congo.

2. INFLATION

Even though President Buhari's propaganda machine has continued to deceive Nigerians that inflation has gone down, Nigerians know that the last time they enjoyed single-digit inflation was under the administration of former President Goodluck Jonathan. There is absolutely no way that the government will increase the price of petrol by over 67% and devalue the currency by over 60% and not expect that inflation will be anywhere below 50%. It is the height of foolery and deceit when President Buhari tries to convince Nigerians that inflation is going down. It is clear that the President is clearly out of tune with the reality on the ground and his only concern is to read the deceitful speeches written by his propaganda machinery.

> *It is the height of foolery and deceit when President Buhari tries to convince Nigerians that inflation is going down. It is clear that the President is clearly out of tune with the reality on the ground and his only concern is to read the deceitful speeches written by his propaganda machinery.*

3. EXTERNAL DEBT

According to Nigeria's Debt Management Office, our total debt as at June 2018 is N22.4 Trillion, compared to 2015 figure which stood at N12.12 trillion. This means that President Buhari has borrowed a total of N10.28 Trillion in three years of being in power. President Buhari and his team are clearly oblivious of the efforts of former President Obasanjo in achieving debt relief. Otherwise, they would have applied brakes in plunging the Nation into another avoidable debt burden. Records from the DMO confirm that the Buhari government borrowed N1 Trillion within the first few months of

> *According to Nigeria's Debt Management Office, our total debt as at June 2018 is N22.4 Trillion, compared to 2015 figure which stood at N12.12 trillion. This means that President Buhari has borrowed a total of N10.28 Trillion in three years of being in power. President Buhari and his team are clearly oblivious of the efforts of former President Obasanjo in achieving debt relief. Otherwise, they would have applied brakes in plunging the Nation into another avoidable debt burden.*

his administration. As it stands, our total debt stock is over $74 Billion.

The future of Nigeria's youths have clearly been mortgaged by this administration as they will be saddled with the responsibility of repaying the debt. It is even more painful when you consider the glaring mismatch between the outrageous debt and infrastructure, production and employment. What is however obvious to Nigerians is that President Buhari's government has totally mortgaged their futures only to pay salaries and fill the pockets of government officials. I'm confident that the day will come when officials of this government will be invited to account for this huge debt burden.

4. ECONOMIC GROWTH

Comparing economic growth under former President Jonathan and current President Buhari is like comparing night and day. Under former President Goodluck Jonathan, CNNMoney named Nigeria as the third fastest growing economy in the world after China and Qatar. But Under President Buhari, Nigeria is now ranked 127th out of 138 countries in the 2016-2017 report by the World Economic Forum (WEF).

S/N	Commodities	Before PMB (N)	Under PMB's Govt. (N)
1	Parboiled Rice (1 bag)	10,000	20,000
2	Beans (1 bag)	18,000	27,000
3	Vegetable Oil (25 litres)	6,500	13,000
4	Yam Flour (1 bag)	40,000	60,000
5	Garri (1 bag)	8,000	12,000
6	Flour	8,000	12,000
7	Sugar	8,800	17,000
8	Semovita (5 kg)	900	1,500
9	Wheat (5 kg)	900	1,500
10	Cooking Gas (12.5 kg)	2,400	3,700
11	Cement	1,500	2,300
12	Kerosene (5 litres)	750	1,125
13	Turkey (1 kg)	800	1,400
14	A Loaf of Bread	70	100
15	A Crate of Eggs	700	850
16	Tomato Paste	40	70
17	A Carton of Indomie	1,400	1,900
18	Airfare Lagos-USA (Economy)	350,000-400,000	600,000-700,000
19	Airfare Lagos-London (Economy)	250,000	400,000
20	Airfare Lagos-Abuja (Economy)	15,000-18,000	30,000-35,000

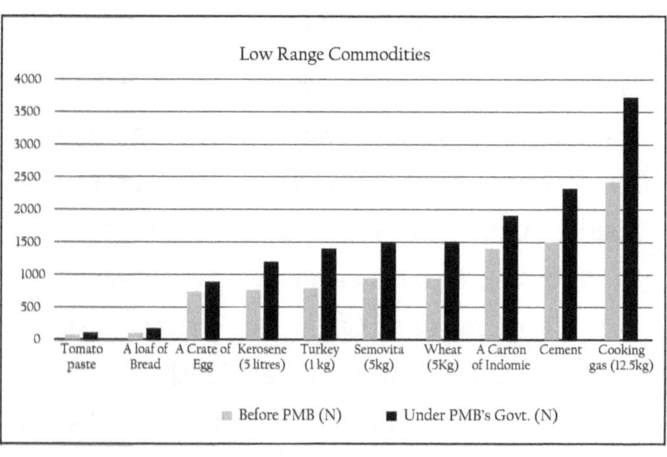

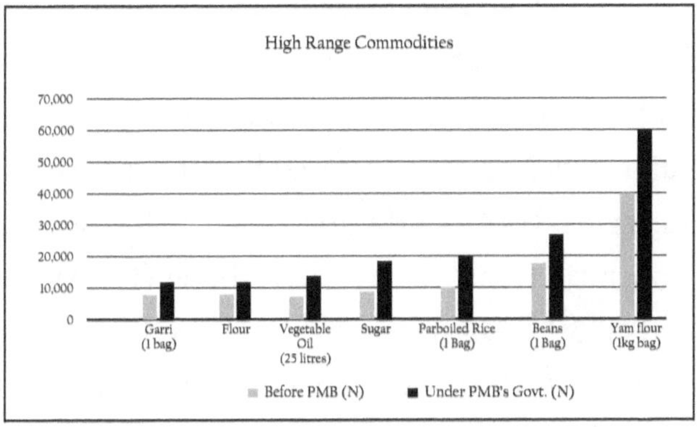

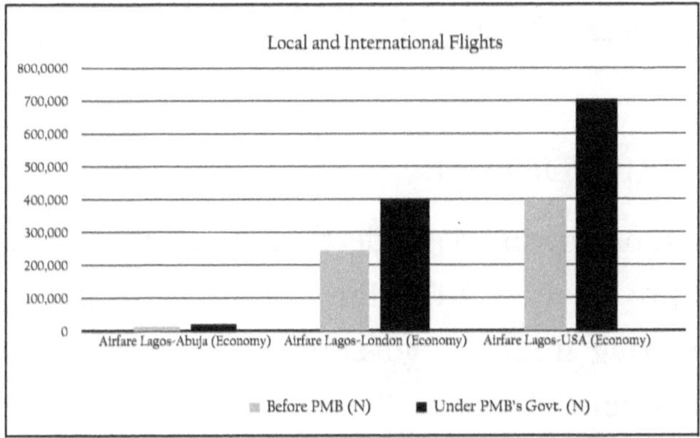

Under former President Goodluck Jonathan, CNNMoney named Nigeria as the third fastest growing economy in the world after China and Qatar. But Under President Buhari, Nigeria is now ranked 127th out of 138 countries in the 2016-2017 report by the World Economic Forum (WEF).

In West Africa, Ghana is ranked 114; Côte d'Ivoire, 99th; Gabon, Cape Verde, 110th; 108th; Senegal, 112nd; Gambia, 123rd; Benin Republic, 124th; and Mali, 125th; Nigeria only fared better than African countries like Madagascar (128th), Congo Democratic Republic (129th), Liberia (131th), and Chad (136th). Below is a survey carried out by the Nigerian Tribune which compares prices of commodities before and after President Buhari took over as Nigeria's President:

5. PRICE OF FUEL

Without giving a single thought to the already impoverished Nigerians who were already suffering from the government's lack of vision, President Buhari's 2016 New Year's gift to Nigerians was to increase petrol pump price from N87 per litre where former President Jonathan left it to N145 per litre. This was despite the fact that one of his major campaign promises was that he would reduce the pump price of petrol. Nigerians will recall that President Buhari's former Minister of Petroleum & Energy when he was a Military Head of State, Prof. Tam David-West, had informed Nigerians that then Candidate Buhari will reduce the fuel pump price from N87 to N40 per litre.

Nigerians will also recall that former President Jonathan had reduced the pump price of petrol from N97 to N87 per litre in January 2015. Apart from late President Umaru Musa Yar'Adua who reduced the pump price of petrol from N70 to N65 per litre, former President Jonathan was the second Nigerian President to reduce the pump price of petrol and both were Presidents under the PDP.

President Buhari had justified the increase by explaining to Nigerians that they had removed the payment of subsidy, only for Nigerians to discover later it was all a lie used by the government to increase pump price because according to them, Nigeria was broke. Nigerians were further shocked that despite the government's claim that they had stopped paying fuel subsidy, they had continued paying to the tune of trillions of Naira.

6. VALUE OF THE NAIRA

It was clear from the onset that Buhari and his team didn't have much clue about how to protect the Naira, plus the irreparable damage done to the Nation's currency by the inability of the President to appoint a capable team to steer the economy in the right direction. The Naira took a dive and the Central Bank being micro-managed by President

Buhari wasn't straightforward, as there were multiple exchange rates for different classes of people, making 'connected' people in Nigeria instant millionaires.

This was alluded to by the Emir of Kano and former Governor of the Central Bank, Mr. Lamido Sanusi, who had warned the government about allowing multiple exchange rates in the country. The value of the Naira today compared to 2015 has been devalued by over 60%, which has made life absolutely difficult for Nigerians and cut the size of the Nation's economy from over $500 billion to probably less than half.

> *The Naira took a dive and the Central Bank being micro-managed by President Buhari wasn't straightforward, as there were multiple exchange rates for different classes of people, making 'connected' people in Nigeria instant millionaires … The value of the Naira today compared to 2015 has been devalued by over 60%, which has made life absolutely difficult for Nigerians and cut the size of the Nation's economy from over $500 billion to probably less than half.*

7. UNABATED FULANI HERDSMEN'S DESTRUCTION OF FARMS AND KILLING OF FARMERS

The 'Fulani' cattle herdsmen have over the years played a significant role by providing our daily supply of beef which still constitutes more than 70% of the animal protein for Nigerians. However, their protracted attacks on innocent farmers and wanton destruction of their crops and residences, has badly affected the production of staple food in many farming communities across Nigeria. What has further aggravated this issue is the absolute helplessness and incapacity of President Buhari's government to bring the situation under control. As a result, wittingly or unwittingly giving tacit approval for criminal elements, brigands and murderers to take the laws into their hands and continue to unleash mayhem in different parts of the country.

News of the nefarious activities of Fulani cattle herdsmen reverberate across the country; from Benue to Taraba, Delta to Edo, Kaduna to Nassarawa, Katsina to Adamawa, etc. The sad reality is that the herdsmen have constituted themselves into a great threat to national food security by their brazen and deliberate destruction of crops resulting in avoidable crises and bloodlettings. Crop farmers across the country are increasingly becoming apprehensive over the negative attitude of the cattle rearers who unleash their herds on the poor farmers' crops, destroying them to points of no redemption. As a result, farmers of cassava, rice, maize, guinea corn and groundnuts now incur extra cost to put hedges around their farms to fend off the marauding cattles whose owners have grown most insensitive to the plights of the average farmer.

DUBIOUS ANTI-CORRUPTION FIGHT

President Buhari refused to learn the right lessons after being ousted by IBB in 1985 as Military Head of State, one of which is the fact that there is a huge difference between fighting corruption and witch-hunting the opposition. In the first place, President Buhari came to power in 2015 on the back of people that he would typically consider corrupt. It was clear that he paid little or no attention to APC campaign funding as he was more concerned with winning the elections than bothering with the source of funding. Can President Buhari say in all honesty and good conscience that all the billions of Naira spent on his campaign was legitimate money? Was it not public knowledge that former Governor of Rivers State allegedly partly sponsored the elections using

> *President Buhari came to power in 2015 on the back of people that he would typically consider corrupt. It was clear that he paid little or no attention to APC campaign funding as he was more concerned with winning the elections than bothering with the source of funding.*

money from Rivers State treasury? And then he was rewarded with a Ministerial Position in the new government.

President Buhari got the whole anti-graft fight wrong from the beginning, as he was unable to understand that there is difference between hounding the opposition and strengthening institutions of government to prevent corruption. President Buhari needed to be reminded that the Economic and Financial Crimes Commission 'EFCC' was a creation of the PDP government. It was clear that the President neither understood the depth of the problems of public corruption nor how to effectively tackle it. True to form, once he took over as President, he immediately started hounding the opposition, throwing them into prison at will and waging a propaganda war using the media.

> *President Buhari got the whole anti-graft fight wrong from the beginning, as he was unable to understand that there is difference between hounding the opposition and strengthening institutions of government to prevent corruption.*

Three and half years down the line, it is clear that the President truly has no real idea or a blueprint on tackling the monster called corruption.

When the coast is clear and Nigeria begins to counts its losses, President Buhari's APC government will probably go down in history as Nigeria's most corrupt government. There are clear signs that many people in this APC government are cleaning out and the President will either be charged as being complicit or totally unaware of the goings-on in his government.

NIGERIA'S DAILY FUEL CONSUMPTION JUMPS TO 65 MILLION LITRES IN ONLY 3 YEARS

It is on record that Minister of State for Petroleum,

Dr. Ibe Kaichukwu, said when the APC came into power in 2015, that Nigeria's daily fuel consumption was in the range of 30 million litres per day. In fact, he questioned that number and said that he believed that it was substantially less than that. Fast forward to 2018 and the NNPC now claims that Nigeria's daily fuel consumption has risen to 65 million litres, blaming the astronomical increase on the rising cases of smuggling of the commodity. This has been disputed by the State governors as being totally outrageous and a plot by NNPC to cut down on its remittances to the federation. Looking at the numbers, the difference between 65 million litres and 30 million litres is 35 million litres. So NNPC and the APC government led by President Buhari is trying to tell Nigerians that we are losing N1.9 Trillion every year to smugglers.

INCREASE OF PETROL PUMP PRICE TO N145 PER LITRE

Even though President Buhari's administration had increased petrol pump price from N87 per litre to N145 per litre, it nevertheless clandestinely continued to pay for fuel subsidy to the tune of N1.4 Trillion. How could a government that is charging extra N58 per litre from the original pump price continue to pay subsidy? The numbers show that by adding N58 to the pump price of petrol and selling 65 million litres per day, the APC government is making N1.4 Trillion extra in revenue over a period of 12 months. Despite making this huge sum of money from the price increase, President Buhari has continued to pay fuel subsidy even when it is unappropriated for by the National Assembly.

CREDIBILITY TEST

President Buhari clearly has many questions to answer and his much-touted integrity is totally overrated. He will equally be held as being complicit when corruption cases that have been established against his close associates have either been played down, totally ignored or swept under the carpet. President Buhari totally failed the integrity test when he failed to take action following the implication of Babachir Lawal, former Secretary to the Government of the Federation, in a grass cutting contract scandal. President Buhari also failed to act promptly when Ayo Oke, former Director of the National Intelligence Agency, was found with $43 million.

Apart from these, President Buhari totally turned a deaf ear and blind eye when his Chief of Army Staff, Lt. Gen. Tukur Buratai, was implicated by Sahara Reporters about unexplained assets in Dubai.

NNPC'S ILLEGAL CONTRACT OF $25 BILLION

Of all the corruption scandals that have rocked President Buhari's government, the biggest is the $25 Billion allegations of abuse of contract awards made by Minister of State for Petroleum, Ibe Kaichukwu, against the Group Managing Director of the NNPC, Maikanti Baru. President Buhari simply dismissed the allegations and did nothing about it. How can the President simply dismiss such allegations made in writing by his Minister of State?

CHAPTER

8

THE PRESIDENT NIGERIA NEEDS

I must state unequivocally that Nigeria has a systemic, fundamental and foundational problem which we have inherited from our founding fathers. For instance, we run a bicameral legislature that is arguably the most expensive in the world. We spend nearly 80% of our budget on recurrent expenditure that has no bearing on 97% of Nigeria's population. In actual sense, only politicians and public servants benefit from the 80% and become stupendously rich for doing nothing. In the first nine months of President Buhari's administration, Nigeria spent over N2 Trillion importing petrol. That amount represents one third of the country's annual budget. We're supposedly the seventh largest exporter of oil in the world but the entire country is in total darkness

> *In the first nine months of President Buhari's administration, Nigeria spent over N2 Trillion importing petrol. That amount represents one third of the country's annual budget. We're supposedly the seventh largest exporter of oil in the world but the entire country is in total darkness without power and majority of Nigerians live in extreme poverty.*

without power and majority of Nigerians live in extreme poverty.

Changing Nigeria is impossible without changing the system and let no one be under the illusion that a miracle can happen. It doesn't matter who becomes the President. You cannot build an edifice on a faulty foundation. It is obvious that changing Nigeria is clearly more than just having a ceremonial constitutional review. When I talk about system, it is more than the constitution. It is a complex and complicated situation that affects the very existence of our Nation. Nigeria, as it is today is unlikely to go far and that is not a curse because everyone wishes the country well.

If a builder or architect told you that your building

has a structural problem, what would you do? You're unlikely to try and repair it because that will be futile and utterly stupid. The building needs to be demolished and rebuilt, so that the foundational problem can be corrected, once and for all. It would seem impossible to rectify a structural problem while the building still stands. It must be brought down. The option is to keep it and try to manage it so that it doesn't fall. That is the situation of Nigeria.

Clearly, we cannot demolish the building called Nigeria. So, we are left with the option to repair and patch and try to make it work. Even if you brought the best architect in the world, he or she would only try to patch and repair and spray some paint here and there. Nothing significant or structural can be done on a building with a faulty foundation. The long-term solution is to bring the whole building down and rebuild.

Over the years, these structural problems have been further exacerbated by weak and inept leadership. So, whoever aspires to be the President of Nigeria must first be aware of these limitations which have created other challenges. He or she must know the constraints that have been imposed on him or her that make it difficult to make lasting change in the system and in the lives of ordinary Nigerians. Be that as it may, the following are the minimum requirements Nigerians expect from any person who is aspiring to be the President of Nigeria:

LIVE BY EXAMPLE

The President of Nigeria must be willing and ready to live by example in ensuring that the entire Aso Villa and all the houses that are occupied by government officials do not have generators. The reason for this is that the president must feel the pain of the ordinary Nigerian, who sometimes do not have power for a calendar month and is unable to afford a generator. The second and most important reason is that the urgency of the situation can only be felt if the President himself is in darkness. Of course, there must be a Power road-map, but the President can only take it seriously if he experiences the same inconveniences as an ordinary citizen of Nigeria.

BE EDUCATED

The President of Nigeria must have at least a university education. This is despite the fact that the constitution of the Federal Republic of Nigeria, recommends secondary school as a minimum qualification. It would appear that the framers of the constitution did not envisage a time when there will be this many Nigerians from every corner of the country who have attained university education. It must be emphasised that having a university education, supposedly provides the candidate with a better and broader world-view. The president's world-view is important because he must understand that the world is bigger than his compound, clan, religion or ethnicity. There is a way leaders who are not so educated view the world and we do not want our President's view of the world to be narrow and parochial.

> *It must be emphasised that having a university education, supposedly provides the candidate with a better and broader world-view. The president's world-view is important because he must understand that the world is bigger than his compound, clan, religion or ethnicity.*

INVEST IN SOCIAL SERVICES AND USE THEM FOR SELF AND FAMILY

The President of Nigeria must be willing and ready to invest in social services from day one in office. This would mean that neither he, his family nor his ministers will be allowed to travel abroad for medical treatment. He would only be interested in fixing the hospitals in the country if he or she knows that his life and that of his or her children depend on their functionality. He and his ministers will also be morally bound to send their kids to government schools and universities in Nigeria, so that they can feel the pain when public schools are shut down and kids have to stay at home, sometimes, indefinitely.

DECLARE ASSETS

The President of Nigeria must be willing to declare his assets from day one so that Nigerians know what their President is worth. He must compel his ministers to do same and all this must be within the public domain so in the event of dishonesty, Nigerians are the first to know. This introduces an element of transparency into government as people know that they will be required to publicly declare their assets when they are leaving office. Nigerians want a President who tells them that he will be content to live off his pension as ex-president and that he doesn't need to embezzle any money. He doesn't need to have foreign accounts as all his kids are here in Nigeria and attend public schools.

MERIT AND NOT NEPOTISM

The President of Nigeria must be ready and willing to take his ministers through a competitive process so that Nigeria can have the benefit of having the brightest and best as their servants. The first major task of the President is to engage the services of a reputable Consultancy firm to advertise the roles of the ministers so that all eligible Nigerians can apply and go through a competitive interview process. This will finally put to bed the whole problem of a President hiring only people from his backyard or people who belong to his religion or ethnic group. It must be made clear from the start that only the best will be hired, irrespective of their religious beliefs or ethnicity.

REDUCE NASS TO ONE CHAMBER AND PART-TIME LEGISLATORS

The President of Nigeria and the party he belongs to must work together to achieve two main objectives with Nigeria's parliament. First, we must collectively agree that at this stage of Nigeria's development, we do not need a bi-cameral legislature. So we must work towards ensuring that we have only one house in the Parliament. Second, we must work towards ensuring that parliamentarians work on a part-time basis and only get paid when they sit and based on the number of bills which are passed. In the long term, this is intended to drastically reduce the cost of running government so that government policies can benefit the ordinary Nigerian.

ENSURE FAIRNESS IN RESOURCE ALLOCATION

The President of Nigeria must be ready and willing to ensure that he sponsors a bill to the parliament that creates a balance in the six geo-political zones of Nigeria. Since local governments are the basis for resource allocation, we must be ready to deal with this issue once and for all. We must be willing to answer difficult questions such as why does Kano have 40 local governments and Lagos has only 20 when they are about the same in population? This may well be the first step towards the much-talked about and contentious restructuring.

STATE OF RESIDENCE AND NOT STATE OF ORIGIN

The President of Nigeria must be ready and willing to ensure that he sponsors a bill to the parliament to the effect that State of Origin, is replaced with State of Residence after people have been resident in that State for a number of years. In the same vein, Nigerians should be indigenes of the States where they are born and not where their parents come from. This will go a long way in reducing friction and cementing the bonds of our nationhood.

NO SPONSORSHIP OF PILGRIMAGE

The President of Nigeria must be ready and willing to ensure we do not pay money for people who are going to Jerusalem or Mecca to pray as we are neither a Christian nor a Muslim country. We are a secular country. People who wish to go on pilgrimages should go at their own expense and not at the expense of Nigeria. Money budgeted for these purposes should be used for social investments that benefit every Nigerian. It must be clear to the President that playing the religious card is at the expense of development and we will never be developed as long as religion plays a major role in the country. While praying is good, it must be clear that it is not prayer that develops a country but enterprise and investments in key infrastructure.

ROAD-MAP FOR INFRASTRUCTURAL REVOLUTION

The President of Nigeria must be ready and willing to develop and defend a road-map for critical infrastructure such as local refineries, roads, railways, social services, etc. He must be able to show that he is willing to create the needed confidence in the economy including an enabling environment for people to invest in key infrastructure in order to create employment. He should demonstrate his willingness to remove subsidies in sectors so that markets and competition can determine the prices of these commodities and services.

It is clear that we have these kinds of people in

THE CHOICE BEFORE NIGERIANS IN 2019 ELECTIONS

The battle-line has been drawn between President Muhammadu Buhari and former Vice President, Atiku Abubakar as they fight for the soul of Nigeria in the forthcoming 2019 elections. In many ways, this election is hugely significant because it will be the first time in Nigeria's chequered history that a former ruling party will try to wrestle power back.

After President Muhammadu Buhari vehemently denied all his electoral promises and having performed woefully, Atiku Abubakar's announcement as the Presidential candidate of the People's Democratic Party has come with great excitement as people are eager and, in a hurry to send Buhari back to Daura. There is a renewed hope that indeed, Nigeria can be delivered from the

> *After President Muhammadu Buhari vehemently denied all his electoral promises and having performed woefully, Atiku Abubakar's announcement as the Presidential candidate of the People's Democratic Party has come with great excitement as people are eager and, in a hurry to send Buhari back to Daura. There is a renewed hope that indeed, Nigeria can be delivered from the clutches and stranglehold of the APC government and the utterly disappointing Buhari administration.*

clutches and stranglehold of the APC government and the utterly disappointing Buhari administration.

But the ruling party is quick to point Atiku Abubakar out as a corrupt politician and that he cannot be trusted with the Nation's treasury. Unbeknownst to them, Nigerians are wiser and know that until about a year ago, Atiku Abubakar was a part of the APC and that they are only trying to paint him black because they know that he is going to give President Buhari a run for his money in the quest to occupy Aso Rock Presidential Villa.

It is public knowledge that Atiku Abubakar has excelled in his private life and successfully run his private businesses, unlike the incumbent President Buhari who had 150 cows in his farm for many years. Atiku Abubakar is probably the second highest employer of labour in Nigeria next to Aliko Dangote. Therefore, Nigerians consider him as capable, competent, cosmopolitan and fully detribalized.

There is an overwhelming weight of evidence to suggest that, given the opportunity to be the President of Nigeria, Atiku Abubakar will do a far better job than the incumbent President Buhari who has shown that he is grossly incompetent, nepotistic and unable to accept responsibility for anything.

It is clear that the President's wife, Mrs. Aisha Buhari is shouting from 'the other room' about the incompetence of the husband and the ruling party. She has used every forum including the unconventional interview she granted to the BBC where she said that she will not be supporting her husband's second-term bid. Mrs. Buhari has also maintained her attacks on the ruling party APC and the Presidency using her Official Twitter accounts @aishambuhari. Below is an example of her tweets where she launched attacks on the ruling party, APC's leadership:

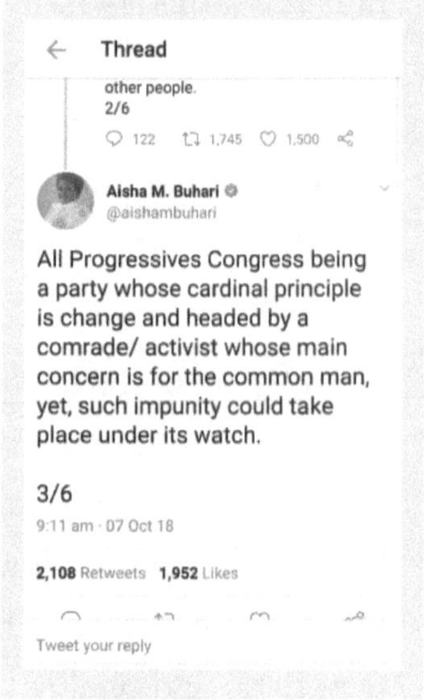

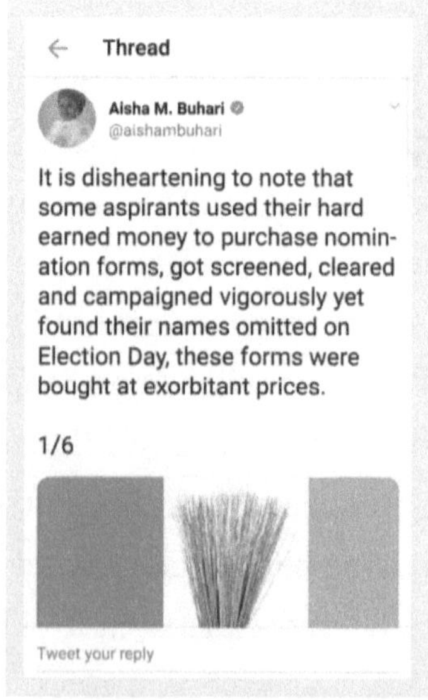

It is public knowledge that Atiku Abubakar has excelled in his private life and successfully run his private businesses, unlike the incumbent President Buhari who had 150 cows in his farm for many years. Atiku Abubakar is probably the second highest employer of labour in Nigeria next to Aliko Dangote. Therefore, Nigerians consider him as capable, competent, cosmopolitan and fully detribalized.

There is an overwhelming weight of evidence to suggest that, given the opportunity to be the President of Nigeria, Atiku Abubakar will do a far better job than the incumbent President Buhari who has shown that he is grossly incompetent, nepotistic and unable to accept responsibility for anything.

2019 PRESIDENTIAL ELECTION BATTLE-GROUND

The real battle-ground for the 2019 Presidential Elections in Nigeria will not be the cliché that Atiku Abubakar is corrupt or that President Buhari isn't corrupt but it will be fought based on the track records of performance and understanding of how the economy works. The fact is that Nigerians have been fooled before by fake promises from the APC government and are unlikely to fall for another set of fake promises. The excitement in Nigeria and amongst Nigerians is a clear testimony to the fact that they are willing to give Atiku Abubakar a chance having shown that he understands business and economics. Nigerians also believe that Atiku Abubakar will be unlikely to divide the country along the sensitive lines of religion and ethnicity.

It is clear that President Buhari does not have the answer to the yearnings and aspirations of Nigerians, as we have never had it this tough in our collective existence as a people. It is time we regain our respect and honour in the comity of Nations, as it is clear that President Buhari is unable to represent us either at home or abroad. What is facing Nigeria and Nigerians today is a choice between proceeding with the poverty that

President Buhari has unleashed on us or giving Atiku Abubakar the chance to lift us from the miry clay to a solid ground where we can collectively aspire to fulfil our destiny as a Nation.

> *It is clear that President Buhari does not have the answer to the yearnings and aspirations of Nigerians, as we have never had it this tough in our collective existence as a people. It is time we regain our respect and honour in the comity of Nations, as it is clear that President Buhari is unable to represent us either at home or abroad. What is facing Nigeria and Nigerians today is a choice between proceeding with the poverty that President Buhari has unleashed on us or giving Atiku Abubakar the chance to lift us from the miry clay to a solid ground where we can collectively aspire to fulfil our destiny as a Nation.*

ABOUT THE AUTHOR

Martins O. Itua is President and CEO, Youth & Women Initiative Africa (YOWIA), an organisation that focuses on changing the narrative on Africa from that of a continent that is blighted by diseases and poverty to one where young people and women take their future in their hands, thereby building a continent that is virile, strong, prosperous and filled with opportunities.

The proactive author of *How the Hell Did I Get Here: Communication, Sex, Money & Divorce - A Candid Perspective* and founder and publisher of *Financial Freedom*, a bi-weekly financial newsletter and online journal, Martins career spans nearly two decades covering the domain of Information Technology, Banking and Finance, Investment

Management and Financial Advisory for individuals and government entities.

With a Master's Degree in Business Administration from the University of Aberdeen, Martins, amongst other things, is now focused on providing entrepreneurial development for the next generation of African business thinkers and leaders. A core believer in global citizenship and making meaningful contribution wherever he finds himself, Martins, while studying in the United Kingdom was an officer cadet in the British Army.

Presently, he lives in Abuja, Nigeria.